# ONLY IN AMERICA

*Aishah Rahman*

I0140511

**BROADWAY PLAY PUBLISHING INC**
New York
www.broadwayplaypub.com
info@broadwayplaypub.com

ONLY IN AMERICA
© Copyright 1997 Aishah Rahman

Cover photo of Aishah Rahman by Berge Ara Lobian

First published by B P P I in *Plays By Aishah Rahman* in February 1997
This edition: July 2019
I S B N: 978-0-88145-857-2

Book design: Marie Donovan
Page make-up: Adobe InDesign
Typeface: Palatino

For Ruba and Stephanie Barry


IN MEMORIAM

Theodora Louis
Yvette Hawkins
Judy Dearing

In order to truly confront a real experience add all the possibilities—what it has been, everything it has been, what it could be, even what it could not be. In other words, the imaginary must be at the very basis of the constitution of what is real.

*Alain Robbe-Grillet*

In order to confront and comprehend a horrifying experience, a woman must add to that event what it has been, everything that it has been, what it could be, and what it could not be. She must never forget to be ashamed to admit that "It is what it ain't what it seems to be."

*Aishah Rahman*

# CHARACTERS & SETTING

CASSANDRA, *she understands words but cannot speak*
ORAL, *a man with a relentless laugh*
LILLI, *a fair warrior*
SCATWOMAN, *a cleaning lady*

*All the characters except* LILLI *are African-American.*


## TIME

*Latter part of the Twentieth Century*


## PLACE

CASSANDRA'*s office on The Hill, U S A*

# ACT ONE

(CASSANDRA's *executive office. A huge sign announces "Animal Bureau of Civil Rights." There is a desk with endless manila folders and a coffee maker. The office is full of various stuffed birds and animals that clutter the space.*)

(CASSANDRA *enters, turns on the radio, and dances and lip synchronizes perfectly to Aretha Franklin's "Respect." The routine is full of humor and she forms her words by moving her lips in an exaggerated fashion. LILLI appears in the wings carrying a doctor's black bag. She watches her dance for a few minutes before she enters.*)

LILLI: (*Snaps the radio off, goes to a closet, pulls out a massage table which she places front and center.*) Who's in a good mood today? Wha happen? Get lucky last night?

CASSANDRA: (*Smiles at* LILLI *as she undresses*) Lohi.

LILLI: (*Inspects her own hands slowly and carefully*)
Hello, Cassandra, not "Lohi." Say it with me slowly, "Hello."

CASSANDRA: (*Points to* LILLI)
Tu nable strin de
Sary qui cri "elo"
Je be Hagarschile
soun lak "Lohi."

LILLI: This is America, Girlfriend.
Got to get down with the lingo.

CASSANDRA: (*Smiles at* LILLI *as she lays down on the massage table and pulls a sheet over her*) Lohi. Lohi. Lohi.

(*Resignedly,* LILLI *removes vials and bottles from her bag, sniffing them as* CASSANDRA *speaks from under her sheet.*)

CASSANDRA: Un menterie fuh to fais rire
Fuh to mak yuh frou frou
Shorpants a un cro-cro lak so
Long assis jes lak un ane!

LILLI: *(Laughing as she snatches* CASSANDRA's *sheet from her)*
That's not the way I heard it. The way I heard it it was the midget
that told his blind date I may be short but I'm long!

*(Both women laugh.)*

CASSANDRA: *(Looking at the bottles)*
Cuandero
Foh se? whafonow?
Gyardan Sass?
Proviso?
Doesta salapetkie?
Dieu Saint anne prochaine
Allatime Saam saam ting?

LILLI: *(Turning* CASSANDRA *over)*
Whatever it takes
As long as it takes
Your lunch hour massage and speech therapy session. Turn over.

*(*CASSANDRA *turns on her stomach.)*

LILLI: *(Pouring contents of all the bottles on* CASSANDRA*)*
Oils, creams, salves, and ointments. Lotions, potions,
panaceas, and remedies. Body balm linements and spirit ease.

*(Begins massaging* CASSANDRA*)*

CASSANDRA: *(Purring like a cat)*
Mmm
Lahd! Lahdooooo muuuusie
Aaa mussie pon misoul
SooogoooooodoooooooyeSSSsss!

LILLI: *(Wearily, as she massages* CASSANDRA*)* Yes, I know.

CASSANDRA: Shofuff bon, shonuff bon shonubonn AHHhhh!

LILLI: You say that all the time.

CASSANDRA: *(Lulled by* LILLI's *hands)*
Whooosh starrry LeeeeLaaaaa.

LILLI: If my fingers feel that good to you how come they don't have
enough magic in them to make you talk?

CASSANDRA: *(Angrily)*
Ama nama

ky seema Yakara
boop-boop boop!

LILLI: You are not!

CASSANDRA: Ana hokay nay!
Je dam so!

LILLI: Look, you can get mad, you can get sad, or you can get glad,
as long as you open your mouth and let me know. After all this time
I want some results from you. I rush over here in lunch-hour traffic
and almost get killed by some hulking maniac who—

CASSANDRA: (Worriedly)
Bandit mash she up?
Almos goh chop she?
Offed? Tuv? YyyyyY?
Offed? Noooooooo.

LILLI: That's right. And only by the power of my loud and dirty fast
and furious mouth did I escape certain death. I was driving across
town when BAM! the car in front of me is suddenly frozen and
I'm practically in the middle of its front seat. I look up and see this
hulking volcano with a bald head, bare chest, and a nipple pierced
straight through with a heavy gold earring marching toward me.
He points to his fender that looks like an accordian and yells,
"Look what you did to my car. You bitch." One look at his pierced
nipple and I knew I had a maniac on my hands. He grabs me by my
throat, bends back my neck like this.... (She demonstrates as she talks.)
Believe me your whole perspective changes when some has their
hands on your throat, bending your head back like this. Your lights
go off even tho' your brain is still on, your world is suddenly upside
down.

(CASSANDRA jumps from under her sheet, a ball of fury, yelling, screaming
and giving karate kicks and chops to LILLI's "attacker.")

LILLI: (Sparring with CASSANDRA) I'll tell you what I did. I let him
have it with my most lethal weapon. MY MOUTH! With words from
A to Z, I shot him. Right between the eyes I blasted him with, "You
Asinine Bovine Cockeyed Demented Elephantine Funkified Grizzly
Halitosis Idiotic Jive Kitty Lecherous Megalomanic Nasty Ossified
Pompous Puffed-up Rancid Slimy Tainted Unwashed Xenophobic
Zit, LET GO OF ME! He let go of me, fell back wounded, bleeding
from his ears, going down for the count, and as the crowd cheered
he whined, "But what about my car?"

"Sir," I said "you can always get another car but you better be on the lookout for ellaplukus."

"What the hell is ellaplukus?" he asked.

"Ellaplukus," I replied, as I drove away, "is when you car get so fucked up, you nipples get infected, and you look in the mirror and see an asshole!"

(CASSANDRA *and* LILLI *crack up.*)

LILLI: My motto is a silent woman is a defenseless woman.

(CASSANDRA, *climbing back on the table, remains silent.*)

(*Silence*)

LILLI: (*Resuming her work*) Open your legs, if you don't talk you're going to die. Breathe deeply. Speak. Raise your arm. Speak. Stretch. Flex, speak. Inhale, Speak... Raise your other arm. Speak.

(*Silence*)

LILLI: I massage every inch of you, eyes, thighs, nipples, dimples, moles, buttocks, pelvis, pudendum, in an effort to get you to make words. Speak, dammit, speak!

(*Silence*)

LILLI: Talk!

(*Silence*)

LILLI: Speak to meeeeeeeee. Oh God, now I'm sounding like you.

(CASSANDRA *reaches for notepad.*)

LILLI: DON'T WRITE. TALK! Thoughts get diluted from brain to pen. Writing slows everything down.
Thoughts get diluted as they travel from brain to pen. Writing isn't as spontaneous as speech.
(*Does a mocking waltz step*)
Think one-two. Write one-two.
Speech is spontaneous as the purest jazz. Just let the words flooooow, girl. Let it floooow.

CASSANDRA: (*Her cooing changes to babbling the following*)
MA, MU, DA, DI, ma. mu, da, di, mamudadi.
Mammadui sssssttt! Mammadudi! Nooooooo! Ecc000k!

LILLI: You had the same dream again?

LILLI: The same one?

CASSANDRA: Ra.

LILLI: The same dream.

CASSANDRA: *(Makes bubbles and spits like a small child trying to form words)* Shickalack wooo apin to ol' HannahWoooo woo.

LILLI: You are driving up a mountain.

CASSANDRA: Cuffy strowing mipath.
Cuffy strowing mipath likeso!

LILLI: You meet a man who is standing in the road.

CASSANDRA: HahhhYaaan se se Ha! See-yah-nah-yuh-see.

LILLI: You slow down? You try to avoid hitting him but you can't?

CASSANDRA: *(Indicates collision with her hands and voice)*
EeeehhhahBammbambam
Nah-see-yuh-nah-nah- nah
NaaaaHannnnnnnNannnnnnnnanaaa.

LILLI: Finally you just close your eyes.

CASSANDRA: *(Continuing to "speak" as she beats her own breasts, abdomen, and genital areas with a high shivering voice)*
Ettite, ettite, ettite
Tee-yah-sah-nah-yah.

LILLI: All the time you still are clutching your steering wheel but your car has disappeared.

CASSANDRA: Tief! Tief! Qui a tiefdecar?

LILLI: You scream over and over, Politicians! Politicians!

CASSANDRA: Negado! Resperado! Ouwanga
ah-nah-kee-yah-tah-nah
see-yuh-nah-yuh-see.

LILLI: The louder you scream the more invisible you become? You are so frightened that you wake up but you can't.

CASSANDRA: *(Continuing to "speak" with a high shivering voice as she beats her own breasts, abdomen, and genital areas)*
Ettite, ettitte, ettitte
Tee-yah-sah-nah-ya

ah-nah-kee-yah-tah-nah
see-yuh-nah-yuh-see.

LILLI: You slow down? You try to avoid hitting him but you can't?

CASSANDRA: Grahhh dahhhhhhhhhhJaaaaa
HeeeeSeeeeeeeee Ooooooooo.

LILLI: (*Her face and body are transformed while she is in the throes of interpretation.*)
You are being attacked.
Body, Mind, and Spirit
Dissected.
You have some control
But not enough.
You are trying, trying, trying to gain control.
The man won't get out of the way,
But he won't hear you.
Your voice is too deep,
Beyond his range.
On his scale of hearing,
His ears only pick up high soprano sounds.
And not your deep, alto warning cries.

(CASSANDRA *and* LILLI *together:*)

| CASSANDRA: | LILLI: |
|---|---|
| Na pas savon qui tace blnc peau | In only your dreams |
| You Pou Pou | dare you speak clearly |
| Awake, a language | Awake, Mas Talk |
| | Language of |
| Nah Nadinola | Disguise, Secret Codes |
| | A Language of women |
| | Of the Afrospora |

Nah bonestrait
Nah acibaaths
Ye mi jisti d eloge
Nah ecoute me me.

LILLI: STOP! NO MORE! DON'T ASK ME.

CASSANDRA: (*Softly, sadly*) Brrrt, brrrrrr hmmmmmm.

LILLI: (*As she quickly gathers her bottles and prepares for exit*)
Listen, Cassandra, I've been called many different names by many
kinds of people. I prefer to think of myself as a Renaissance woman,

a masseuse by vocation, a therapist by training, clairvoyant through revelation, a musician by avocation, a lover by inspiration, and a rascal by my nature. But I am not your mouthpiece. Your dreams and nightmares need your voice not mine. Your dreams need your voice, not mine.

CASSANDRA: *(Angrily)* Brrrrit Sssstha ccuuuuuruuu.

LILLI: Any port in a storm? Is that so. Well this sailor is jumping ship! *(Puts bottles back in bag)* Tough tittie sugar. Lili's going. Lunchtime massage is over.

*(CASSANDRA glares at LILLI silently as she pecks her on the cheek.)*

LILLI: You used to talk. What stopped you?

CASSANDRA: *(Argumentatively, trying to delay LILLI's exit)*
Brrrrt sssstuuuuuuuuucuuuuuuuu
Ssssssst Sssst Stttttt Brrru
Ra
*(She twitters.)*
Chuu Upp TwwwiUp Chhht! EeeuU.

LILLI: No kidding?

CASSANDRA: *(Gurgles)* Cuuuuuduuu Ruuu.

LILLI: You don't say?

CASSANDRA: RuuuuuuuGuuu Oooooo.

LILLI: I see said the blind man to the deaf woman.

CASSANDRA: Doh me we feeee.

LILLi You sound like the Greek princess whose tongue was ripped out before she was changed into a swallow.

CASSANDRA: *(Grows angry)* Fuuuuu uuuuuuuu ckuuu Dooo!

LILLI: *(Laughing)* Now, now.

CASSANDRA: *(Pleadingly)* Salalch slacha soute sa? Eeeese?

*(LILLI silent)*

CASSANDRA: *(Pleads)* BuuuuuUuuuu LuuuuNu?

LILLI: No more. Can't understand you. Bye Bye. Remember, Cassandra. Speak American.

(CASSANDRA *stares at* LILLI's *exiting back. She angrily gets dressed, carrying out a conversation with herself in which she mocks* LILLI. *She jumps involuntarily at the sight of* ORAL.)

ORAL: (*Laughs a deep, rich, long laugh as a way of announcing his presence. Carries a huge, empty cage. Greets* CASSANDRA *with a waist-deep bow.*) Ms Jackson.

CASSANDRA: (*Smiles at* ORAL *a little too brightly*) Lohi.

ORAL: (*Laughing as he enters*) This is top secret. We've got an endangered coming in. This cage is for The Giant American Horned Lizard. Commonly known as the Horny Toad. Our job is to figure out how to propagate the species. The Bureau's secret mission is to Multiply! Capture! Multiply! Manufacture! From the Horny Toad we get D D T, plastics, tie clips, cigarette holders, and jelly beans. The Horny Toad is good for industry. Good for America. The Animal Bureau for Civil Rights received a mandate from You-know-where. Keep this classified. The You-know-whos would picket. The You-know-whats would boycott. A A S P C A and all the other alphabets would howl. They have their heads tied on backwards. They got to be dragged, screaming and kicking, into the 21st century. (*He places the cage among the other specimens.*) How was your session today? No improvement? I'm not surprised. No wonder. You could have any doctor in the country and yet you insist on that...that WOMAN...that...that NEW AGE QUACK.... That...that...

CASSANDRA: (*Smiling, writes on her notepad, and hands it to him*)
Her. Sistren de moi
ha Ra. Ra. Good.
Ami cheri. Booon.

ORAL: (*Laughing as he reads*) That's exactly what I mean. What about me? I've been more of a help to you than that WOMAN could ever be, haven't I? Aren't you sitting in the top echelons of power? Huh? Aren't you? Despite your handicap? Huh? Didn't I help mainstream you? Huh? Didn't I?

(CASSANDRA, *still smiling, pours him a cup of coffee. He takes a long, relaxing sip, never taking his eyes away from her*)

ORAL: Ahhhhhhh. A perfect cup of coffee. Mmmmmmm...
Did you hear my speech before the Knights today?

CASSANDRA: (*Shaking her head from side to side*) Uh-uh.

ORAL: *(Laughing)* I was good. You should have heard me.
You should have seen me. In that hall, up on that stage, addressing
the most influential men in America, looking down into their rich
and powerful eyes, I tell you Ms Jackson, I was Jesus standing before
the multitude. It...was...a...a transcendent moment.
*(Assumes oratorical pose and voice)*
Fellow Knights. The American people have a great history! We must
all step in unison, straight legged and stiff-kneed, to our victorious
and prosperous American destiny to be prosperous and victorious.

*(ORAL laughs as CASSANDRA automatically continues to smile.)*

ORAL: You read about my speech before Congress?
*(Again he assumes oratorical pose and voice:)*
Honored Knights. Throw away your Liberal Guilt and rest assured.
Anything can be justified as a matter of economics and I'm not bitter
and I'm not mad.

*(CASSANDRA continues to smile and continues to pour coffee as ORAL
contorts his body in back-bending, knee-slapping, high-stepping laughter.)*

ORAL: I refuse to be part of an endangered species. I refuse to
become an "X". *(Continues to guffaw)* Know what all those letter Xs
walking around *really* mean? Huh, Ms Jackson? X-tinct! That's what!
*(Laughs hysterically)* That's right. X followed by Z. Zapped out. Zero.
Not even a ghost. Not even a trace. Wiped off the face of the earth.
*(Continues to laugh, cups his hand to his mouth, makes the call of the
carrier pigeon)* BrrrrUuuuuuuCuuuTttttoooooo. Hear that? That was
one of the greatest zoological wonders of the world. Cuuuucuuuuu!
His bird call used to be unique music among birds. See those wings,
muscular, long, dark, graceful, athletic. Twenty-two million of these
elegant birds. Gone. Wiped out! Not by nature but by human beings.
The males were killed off. First the wild ones, corralled in pens
where mass slaughter took place. Then male after male destroyed.
Look at him, this elegant, extinct bird, Ms Jackson. Look.

*(CASSANDRA looks at his empty hand.)*

ORAL: Nada. Zip. You don't see anything, do you?

*(CASSANDRA shakes her head in agreement.)*

ORAL: Of course not, this elegant, extinct bird is gone, Ms Jackson,
wiped out . X-stinct. That's why my hand is empty! That's what ain't
gonna happen to me!

*(CASSANDRA pretends to smile and work.)*

ORAL: Irony. Ms Jackson, Irony. That's what I love best about America. Its great sense of irony. Only in America will you see a man like me at the head of the A B C, the Animal Bureau of Civil Rights in spite of the fact that I HATE ANIMALS! A dog ain't nothing but a toned-down wolf and a cat ain't nothing but a pumped up-rat! Tame or wild, I hate 'em all! Mother Nature should have been a man! He'd know what to do. X 'em all. (*Knocks down several stuffed specimens*) Zap 'em out. X and Z. Open season on all animals. That's an order from Father Nature and Oral Jackson, head of A B C. (*Collapses into laughter*)

(CASSANDRA *buries her head in work.*)

ORAL: (*Knocks a few folders away to get* CASSANDRA'*s attention*) Ms Jackson. STOP WORKING! You're so ambitious!

CASSANDRA: (*Writing furiously; gives to* ORAL)
Cougar fite coudah
mek we time o
drip drip lili stale watah.

ORAL: (*Snatches note from her*)
You say "Dangerous backlog of cases?" To quote Miles Davis...
"So What?" (*He tosses note on the carpet.*)

(CASSANDRA *writes again.*)

ORAL: (*Snatches and reads*) "Animal Rights Organizations Outraged?"
(*Laughingly tosses it to the floor*)

CASSANDRA: (*Writes angrily again as* ORAL *again snatches notes*)
Just ice be beg ging
righteous to do e lind
not blind.

ORAL: (*Snatches note and reads*) "Public outcry." The Public be damned! You don't get it, do you? (*Slowly, as if he is talking to someone who reads lips*) There-are-corporations-behind-me. Powerful-men-who-won't-let-America-be-torn-apart-by-a-backward-liberal-raging-public! (*Again he throws her note on the floor.*)

CASSANDRA: (*Writes on the notepad*)
Un boisyard!
Ma che te! Petella! Chopup!
Chaudin me fait mal chaudin. Urrrrrr!

(CASSANDRA *sucks her teeth and rolls her eyes at* ORAL.)

ORAL: *(Snatches note from her)* Hate crimes? Economic discrimination? Against animals? Oh why must you people always moan and moan, bitch, whine, and moan? *(He tosses the note on the floor.)*

CASSANDRA: *(In a seductively sweet change of tone)*
Mak a miration
bigu smal smal I-O
les quatres paroisse
nown yourn name-O.

ORAL: "We...should...draft...an...Animal...Rights...Law" NEVER!
*(Angrily tosses note on floor)*

CASSANDRA: *(Writes again)*
Pattah roller!
Bountihunta!
Ovahseer!

ORAL: *(Snatches note from her)* Ninety-eight percent of the cases I decide are against animals? What do the beasts expect?

CASSANDRA: *(Writing continually)*
Gopoboodooooh. police
bam sh kill king
sulah free juris pru niggah.

ORAL: You say, "Animals are a historically oppressed group." I say it's their own fault. *(Crumples note before tossing it to floor)* *(Snatching another note)* God don't eat slick, slimy okra? What's that supposed to signify, Ms Jackson? *(Again crumples and tosses the note to floor)* Ms Jackson. I know the liberals, the radicals, the moderates, even the vegetarians are screaming for my male blood. But what care I? I've always acted alone. I'm the cowboy riding ahead. I'm the endangered species determined to survive the howling mob at my heels. Just me and my horse all alone under a wide open sky. All the howling do-gooders can do is eat my dust and stay off my blue suede shoes.

*(CASSANDRA still writing)*

ORAL: STOP YOUR DAMNED SCRIBBLING! I HATE A SCRIBBLING WOMAN!

*(CASSANDRA is frozen into a plastic smile as ORAL extends his empty coffee cup to her and she automatically pours.)*

ORAL: Ms Jackson. I do admire your zeal. A power position on the Circuit is opening up soon. It's you I'll recommend.

*(CASSANDRA's smile returns as she pours coffee all through the following. Neither notices the overflow.)*

ORAL: Ms Jackson. Believe me, I do admire your ambition. Why don't you represent me at the power luncheon on Monday at two P M. You'll be one of twelve guests, six at two tables. You'll be seated next to The Speaker. You'll eat on gold plates and dine on oysters Rockefeller, chestnut soup, pheasant, and champagne. For dessert you'll enjoy chocolate souffle. Are you ready, Ms Jackson?

*(CASSANDRA keeps smiling and pouring.)*

ORAL: *(His voice suddenly husky)* I-am-ready.

CASSANDRA: Brrr. Brrr. Sssst!

ORAL: "He's" ready too.

CASSANDRA: CUUUooooooowouuu!

ORAL: He's been ready.

CASSANDRA: Ssst! Psssst Giiiiiii!

ORAL: He's been waiting.

CASSANDRA: Cuuuuoooowooooou!

ORAL: He's hungry.

*(ORAL whispers in CASSANDRA's ear.)*

CASSANDRA: *(Moves angrily away from him)*
Guuuu. OoOoooOO
CucucuDuuuhhhhh
rahhhhshiiiiiit!

ORAL: Ahhh gal, I love those sexy sounds you make when you try to talk. *(He follows her.)* Giant! You gonna help me find him? Giant wants you to find him. Giant is lonely and Giant is g-ett-i-n-g IMPATIENT!

CASSANDRA: *(Tries to move away from him)*
Ettitte! Ettitttie suuuah!

ORAL: *(Stalks and finally corners her)* Big Giant!

*(CASSANDRA turns her face away from him. At this point she becomes more birdlike in neck and arm movements as well as vocally, as she emits the*

*gurgling, strangled swallow sounds which increase throughout the end of the act.)*

ORAL: *(Stalking and dancing around her throughout to the end of the act)* Don't turn away, Ms Jackson. Ms Jackson. Don't be such a prude. I'm only talking. What harm can words do?

CASSANDRA: *(Circles and glides and soars away from him, trying to escape, and continues to emit harsh, deep, gurgling, sounds)* Bzsaaa zssa zsaaa brrrtt!

ORAL: *(Laughing)* Ms Jackson. Don't get so upset. I'm just talking. Using words. It's a free country and I can talk sexy if I want to. Your tongue may be tied but mine ain't.

CASSANDRA: Brrrtt! brrrtt! brrrtt! brrtt!

ORAL: *(Ominously)* Ms Jackson...I said...take...a look...at GIANT! The womb beater. The deer slayer. The buck binder. The woman finder. The finger sucker. The bed tucker. The cock plucker. The gun slinger. A hum dinger. The pussy ringer. Baby bringer. Cherry picker. A tittie licker. Inside tickler. Big dicker. Giant!

CASSANDRA: *(With rapid, flickering, winglike arms, she peels photos from her body while emitting a harsh, agitated, gurgling sound)* Chwew, churr, chewew churr brrrtt brrtt brrrrt brrtbrt Un bajoe! buckro! mamaguay

ORAL: My tied-tongue, gurgling, sexy, swallow. *(Dramatically throws up his hands)* Look, Ms Jackson. Rest assured I'm not going to touch you. I want no physical contact. No bodies. No odors. No secretions. No pubic hairs. What I love is smut. A sanitary blending of lechery, sight, and speech. Smut. Visual. Verbal. Hygenic. Each word is a picture. Each picture an orgasm. Smut eases me. Smut makes me happy. You know how I feel when I'm happy? I feel limp and wet all over from Cassandra's tongue. When I'm happy, I am the golden sun god Apollo finally worshipped by his Cassandra. I feel Cassandra's legendary tongue...coated...with...Apollo's gift of prophecy...licking me all over. Iiiiiii...seeeee...the future...in Cassandra's tongue...as it wraps around my Giant and sings Apollo's praises...ohhh. When I am happy, the ceiling of my head lifts annnnnnnd I am golden Apollo sitting on a golden bench wearing a golden robe looking at a Big Mac which I am licking alllll over as it turns into a huge pink breast annnnd I break into golden sunshine annnnd my golden giant pierces a cloud in the sky and out steps Cassandra with her legs

spread wiiiide open with one foot on sunrise the other on sunset
annnnnnnnd her her magic tongue sloooooowly sliiiiiides down
Giant who quivers annnnnnd divers annnnnnd bucks annnd snorts
annnnnnnnnnd sniffs annnd snays annnnnnd annnnnnnnd dookie
annnnd fooooookie nndpoooootie and smookie mookie tiiiiitie
annnnnnnnnAhhhhhhhhhhhh!

*(CASSANDRA flies toward the door.)*

ORAL: DON'T GO! I ABSOLUTELY FORBID IT!

*(His command slows CASSANDRA's flight.)*

ORAL: Where are you running off to? Who are you going to tell?
Ms Jackson. Let's be Shakespearean about this:
"Tis better to be vile than vile esteemed
When not to be received reproach of being,
And the just pleasures lost, which is so deemed.
Not by our feelings, but by others seeing.
For why should others' false adulterate eyes
Give salutation to my sportive blood?"
*(Laughs and laughs)*
In other words, Ms Jackson, I don't give a damn what you or others
say about me. There's nothing wrong in here. I'm only talking,
I'm only talking, I'm only talking, and the evil is in *your* imagination.
And besides, who are you going to tell? The President? Congress?
What are you going to tell them? That I'm the demon they created?
The nightmare of the nation?

*(Her movement toward the door is further slowed by his words.)*

ORAL: Forget about the girls in the front office. Cheryl is on a
fact-finding junket to Las Vegas with Senator Snow. Celia's with
Senator Haring on Lobbyist Brown's yacht. My girls are loyal team
players and wouldn't even listen to you. Nobody will listen to you,
Ms Jackson.

*(This completely stops CASSANDRA's flight toward door.)*

ORAL: Know what I think? Giant crawled up your legs. Between your
thighs. Into where it's dark and dirty. Smack dab in the middle of
your hairy, juicy swallow, little bird. My little birdie. That's what I
think.

*(She flies toward door again.)*

ORAL: *(Laughing relentlessly)* MS JACKSON, HALT! Just where
do you think you'll be working after you walk out of this office?
Hamburger helper? Cigarette person? Bus person? Shampoo person?
Greeter? Messenger? Assistant? Aide? Office Girl? Gal Friday?
Off-the-books? Self Starter?

*(Each job he names propels her back into her office until she finally once
again is facing him. ORAL continues to drone on, forcing her backward
in front of the empty cage. She mouths sounds but now none come forth.
ORALs voice continues, relentless, even after the lights are off.)*

ORAL: Nanny? Mammy? Freelance? Hostess? Handywoman?
Telephone gal? Part time? Sitter? Picker? Sorter? Entry level?
Para person? Assistant person?? Trainee? Processor? Operator?
Dispatcher? Check out? Taxi? Tax? Taxi 21st century and still no
Taxi? Heeey Taxi!...

*(From CASSANDRA's throat: the strangled cry of swallows)*

ORAL: *(Flirtatious, contemptuous, lewd, and savage)*
Poor Cassandra
Mute and mewing
Gibble Gabbling incoherently
Begging for interpretation
Gesticulating instead of articulating
In your dumb hot silence
Not feeling
The voluptuousness
The sensuality
of Speech
The fleshy feel of moist Lips wide apart
The hard Teeth
Against the poised, pink, wet Tongue
The Mouth spread wide open
Pulsating vocal cords
Pumping lungs
The ecstastic moment
Before speech
Before piercing through silence
Before pushing the air through
The quivering,
Wet tongue.
The scent of your own breath
Rising in your nostrils

As you open your lips
pouring forth sound
Ejaculating in the air
A jism of words!
Fecund Words,
Steaming
Animals in the brain
Lusting to be born
Seeds germinating in the mind
Waiting to be fed
Vowels thirsting for enunciation
Consonants crying for fruition
Streaming Syllables
Uniting on the tongue
Dumb Cassandra!
Mute and inarticulate
Rigid, frigid,
Virgin mouth,
Can you Imagine,
The taste of "dict—tion—ary" on the tongue
Or "thunderrrrrrrrrrr" roaring and roiling
Whirling and curling, in the belly of your throat
Lustily gathering frothy spit
For you to emit
its Sound?
"Brouhaha" will make you laugh
"Tintinnabulate "tingles
While "spinet" makes you salivate
A warm breath from mouth to ear
Is throaty, velvet "rhapsody"
"Staccato" jumpstarts the tongue
A Word can
hum drum, sing song, jingle jangle, ding dong, jog trot, zig zag and
boogie woogie
In two syllabic alliterative tautologic interminability
A Word will weep and willow and wave
Like a feather in a storm
Or legato on the tongue
Or sillyilly slip and slide
"Eureka" leaps on the lips and gloats
From the rear of your throat
"Crescendo" rises

To the roof of your mouth
"Tiptoe" and "tête-a-tête"
Play tag with tongue and teeth
A Word can
Writhe and wiggle like "wigwam"
Convulse or spasm like "orgasm"
It can swing on the tongue like a "pendulum"
Or put wind in your whistle like a whopping whale
It can rococco your imagination
Spindle your ear
Splinter your infinitive
Sibilate your tongue
Lilt like a licentious Lilliputian lingering lazily on your labia
Give me Sesquipedlian Pollysyallabism
I'll even take balderdash and gobbleygook
My tongue can twist and turn and click and change
Jes es many Words es ah durn please
Yo Word, Word Up, Word to the Motherland,
Wie ghets?
Mah nish ma?
Va bine?
So nu?
Soh si by che tay
To do bien?
Do des ka?
Wha's up?
There is no alien tongue
No foreign speech
The only dead language
is
Silence.

END OF ACT ONE

# ACT TWO

(*Same set.* CASSANDRA *sitting, fearfully watching* ORAL's *every move, growing visibly angry.* ORAL *meticulously picks up each piece of scattered notepaper from the carpet, looks at it, laughs, folds it, and puts it in his pants pocket. He lifts up a chair, sets it sideways, inspecting it carefully. He turns the cluttered desk on its side, then on its back, continuing his search. Satisfied, he carefully tilts the desk back upright. He removes his suit jacket, loosening his tie and shoe laces, unbuttons his shirt.* SCATWOMAN *enters with mop and pail.*)

(SCATWOMAN *cleans by sprinkling dust over objects and polishing them as she sings an eerie, repetitious tune.*)

CASSANDRA: (*Crawls over to* SCATWOMAN *in a frantic, futile attempt to get her attention*)
O ebon ebon miart maria
Ave holi sustria
nah re pects Metria
Bajoe nah ami Wanmia
O ebon miart Miara
gyul ah bawling a yeea
Lahhhhd o mussie 'pon shhhea.

(SCATWOMAN *ignores* CASSANDRA *and keeps on humming and cleaning.*)

ORAL: Hey you! What do you think you're doing?

SCATWOMAN: Cleaning, Sir.

ORAL: With dust? You cleanse with dust?

SCATWOMAN: Mi teethskin ain fren
mi bye-bye ain end
Cuz mi yout ape foot to han
mek we ah crawl to stand
hog dead no water on
mek ah we go dead to live.

ORAL: Am I the only articulate human in this room? What are you babbling about.

SCATWOMAN: Ol' gal trick. Catching dirt with dirt.

ORAL: Oh. I see. I think.

SCATWOMAN: Yes Sir.

ORAL: *(Making up and down motions)* Up and down up and down!

SCATWOMAN: Sir?

ORAL: *(Demonstrating)* No circles! Your motions are all wrong. Can't you see that? Your rhythms are off. It's all in the wrist! Up! Down! Down! Up! Linear Movement. Circles spread filth. Spread in a circle, dirt chases its own dust. Like a snake chasing its own tail!

SCATWOMAN: I'll try, Sir.

ORAL: Try? At your age you should know what I want without my having to coach you.

SCATWOMAN: Just show me how you want it done. Sir.

ORAL: After all these years, you should know. You aren't union, are you?

*(CASSANDRA begins to mock and threaten ORAL behind his back.)*

SCATWOMAN: Oh no, Sir.

ORAL: Good. Read my mind. Anticipate my desires. Don't just stand there. Polish her cage.

SCATWOMAN: Yes Sir.

*(Polishes cage, ignoring CASSANDRA's frantic gestures.)*

ORAL: Stop! Just look at the cage. Just stand there and look at it.

SCATWOMAN: Yes Sir.

*(CASSANDRA continues and tries many times to sneak up on ORAL, but he manages to remain just out of her reach.)*

ORAL: Stand back. Look at it closely. What do you see?

SCATWOMAN: Nothing Sir?

ORAL: That's what's wrong. You look at that cage and see nothing. You're sure you're not union?

SCATWOMAN: Oh no Sir. Yes, Sir.

ORAL: What are you doing? Get off your knees! I didn't ask for that. You sure you aren't union? Who sent you?

SCATWOMAN: Housekeeping, Sir.

*(Continues vigorous polishing as CASSANDRA pulls and tugs at her)*

ORAL: Emma? Mae? No, Rose?...Rose! That's your name. Isn't it?

CASSANDRA: *(Pleading with SCATWOMAN)*
Bele?
Mele?
Ni mi dahtee?
he de banshee!
I av miltyfree
gi tin panky
Bele?
Mele?
O yam dahatee!

SCATWOMAN: Yes Sir. Rose.

ORAL: Rose. There's a fleck of lint on the bars. Right over there.

*(CASSANDRA tugs frantically at SCATWOMAN.)*

ORAL: Rose, do you feel anything?

SCATWOMAN: No, Sir.

CASSANDRA: BELE? MELE? O YAM DAHATEE!

ORAL: Do you see someone?

SCATWOMAN: *(Covers both her eyes)* No Sir.

ORAL: What will you say about...all this?

*(SCATWOMAN covers her mouth.)*

ORAL: Is someone trying to get your attention?

SCATWOMAN: No.

ORAL: Is someone trying to get you to help her?

SCATWOMAN: No.

CASSANDRA: *(Frantically appealing to SCATWOMAN tugging and pulling at her body)*
Naaa. NaaaaaaXoxa Shebon nashun
Naaa. NaaaaaaXoxa! plant ashun!

Naaa. Naaaa. for ation!
Sheba sheba MmmmOoooooooosheban jitah
Maaaaahiiii Jitigah Mahhiit Jitgah
OoooO OooooO.

ORAL: Do you hear someone?

SCATWOMAN: (*Covering both ears with her hands*) No sir.

CASSANDRA: Fugitttttta vox fugiiittt.

ORAL: (*Goes toward her and takes her hand gently*) Don't be so servile.
Act like a human being. For Christ's sake you are a human being
aren't you?

SCATWOMAN: Yes, Sir.

ORAL: Then act like one. You don't have to be afraid of me.
I regard you as a mother.

SCATWOMAN: Yes Sir.

ORAL: Now get the hell out!

(*He chases her out, then laughs and turns to* CASSANDRA, *who is exhausted
with her futile efforts and reverts to swallowlike movements and sounds.*)

ORAL: Ahhhhhhh dear sweet Momma. I love her like an angel,
the devil. My mother is a saint. There is no woman more clean,
more long suffering, more religious, more loyal, more independent,
more faithless, more vicious, more immoral or treacherous.

(SCATWOMAN *re-enters the room with a gleaming gold gold tray on which
are several small roasted swallows.*)

ORAL: WOW! What a feast! Four-and-twenty swallows set before a
king.
(*Tears greedily into the little birds, throws feathers, bones, and skin
randomly around*)
Yum! My favorite delicacy. Roast swallow.

(*Slowly devours the birds one after the other, all the while looking gleefully
at* CASSANDRA's *misery.*)

ORAL: Won't you join me in this delightful feast my birdie? I like
to swallow my swallow in great big swallows.... Don't look at me
in that tone of voice or I'll make you swallow your silent words.
Sometimes, my birdie, you are hard to swallow. You can't swallow
me up and no one is gonna swallow any dirt you say about me so
relax and let's swallow some swallow together! (*He cracks the bones*

*with his teeth and sucks out the marrow, which runs down his jaws, cheeks, and chin, which he licks away.)* Gooooood, Sweeeeet, Tennnnder, Juuuuuicy swallow! *(He breaks off a sparrow's foot and picks his teeth with its claws.)*

SCATWOMAN: *(Enters a trancelike state as her body begins to swing and sway to her inner music)* Shoo-be do ooo ya coo!

ORAL: Stop it. Be still dammit! What the hell do you call yourself doing?

*(SCATWOMAN begins to scat throughout the scene as she cleans, still remaining impervious to all else while addressing the cages, desk, table, chairs, etc that she touches in her work with her song. Although she is scatting, her emotion and meaning should be clear to the audience, as "shoo be doo do" is when Louis Armstrong sings it. Her song is one of pain, endurance, and jubilation, and resembles Betty Carter's "Movin On" without words.)*

SCATWOMAN: *(Cleaning in big circular motions and singing as if her song is a prayer to every object she touches)*
Weeeeee uhhhhhhhhhmovinnnonnnnnaa!
ooooLoooahhhhhgleeeeeweeeeeeuuuhhhh
Scagaaaaajjjjeeeeee uuuuhhhhgooooooota
keeeepppppppppppllaaaaaaaa Ahhhhhhhhhhudedad Onnnnnnnnn
AHhhhhhhhhhudeda nnnnnnooooo *(In swinging rhythms)*

ORAL: Cleaning Woman? Rose? What's gotten into you?
Speak English! You used to speak English.

CASSANDRA: *(To SCATWOMAN)*
O ebon ebon miart mumu
se judu trau tu
Maedure, thu eart on heofonu
si thin nama gehlgodu.

*(CASSANDRA's and SCATWOMAN's voices meld into a duet.)*

CASSANDRA: Amnja Yemya
Mama Oshun
Mamaguy
Hey qui mo i a ma
jaj aj wa Baba
Oyam ya dahatee
u nu thine
aha hahh ahhhh

u nu thine
aha hahhh ahaha
Jumbie ah calling tine
strait de cementine
Shuuuuuuusaaaave me
Mamaguyeeeeeeee.

SCATWOMAN: Boop dee dooo bee haaa
booooobeeee doooowweee doooweee aaa aaaas
eeeeeee
aaaaaaaOOOOOOOayyyyyyy.

*(Duet begins to build ;*ORAL *breaks in.)*

ORAL: SHUT THE FUCK UP! RIGHT NOW!

*(*CASSANDRA *stops abruptly.)*

SCATWOMAN: *(Ignoring* ORAL*)*
Ooooooooshoooobe dooooo OOOooyaaa coooooo!

ORAL: Stop! I'll fire you.

SCATWOMAN: *(Continues)*
Shooooobeeee dooo shoooobeee dooooOoO...
Ooooya coooo ooooya cooo shooooo.
Ooobooop she bammmmoyacoo!

ORAL: I'm warning you, woman! You better straighten up and fly
right!

SCATWOMAN: *(Her voice continues to climb.)*
A body de bop dap dap abodi doo dop de dop

ORAL: YOU'RE FIRED! Fired, fired, fired! Goddamit!

SCATWOMAN: *(Her voice reaches a climax and then lapses into a lullaby
mode as she cleans and seranades whatever her hand touches.)*
ONNNNNNNNnnn nnnnnnn NnnnONNNNNNNN!
YaaaaAAAHH.
Baaaaabeeeeeeeeeahhhhhhhmeeeeohhhhhhbaaaaabeeeebaaaabeeee.

ORAL: *(Appealing to* SCATWOMAN*)*
What are you trying to do me?
*(Appeals to* CASSANDRA*)*
Leave me alone! I'm only a man.

*(His words drive* CASSANDRA *back into the cage.)*

ORAL: *(Stands in front of the cage, yelling)*
I'm surrounded. Lesbians one and all. Watching. Always watching.
Is the Matriarchal Underground out to get me? Is it really the moon
that follows me everywhere or is it the relentless eye of a woman?

SCATWOMAN: OOOOOOOoNooooooooooooOONononononononon
OnNoooooooNoooNo.

CASSANDRA: *(Gasping, spitting, and face contorted with her tremendous
effort to form words)*
NNNN NN NN Nnn nn n nnnn n
nnn nNNN NNNN NNnNNN NNN Nnnnnn.

SCATWOMAN: *(Continues, impervious to CASSANDRA and ORAL)*
GATATATATATKEEPNOOOOOOOONoooooooooNOO!

CASSANDRA: NnnnnnnnNN N N N NNNN!

ORAL: *(Whispering and gesturing surreptitiously in order to hide from
SCATWOMAN)* Look who I've found!

CASSANDRA: BrrrrSttt!

ORAL: Whaddya know. He's been hiding here all along.

CASSANDRA: OOOOOOOOO!
NNnnnnnNNNNN!

ORAL: GIANT!

CASSANDRA: NnnnnnnnnNNNNNNN
OOOOOOOOOooOOOOOOOOOO!

ORAL: GIANT!

CASSANDRA: O! O! O!O!
N! N! N! N!

ORAL: That almost sounds like a word, Ms Jackson.
*(Does a little two-step)*
Let's see if you can speak more clearly...GIANT!

CASSANDRA: NNNNNNNNNNNNNN ahhhhhheeeeeeeeeee
OoooOOOOOOOOOO.

ORAL: Giant can't quite understand you. You must make Giant
understand.

CASSANDRA: NnnnnNNNNNNNNN O Nnnnnnn oooOOo
Nnnnnnnn OOOOO
NnNNNNNNN OHhhhhh EeeeNNNN OOOOOO!

ORAL: I suppose that if you could speak you would appeal to me for Justice? I'll tell you what I know of justice. Although I never committed any crime, Justice is a jury insisting that I confess, that I cry and look repentant before they condemn me. I suppose that if you could speak you would screech to me in strident tones about equality? My dear woman. Do you have any idea what it takes to be a man like me? To be invisible in the world with no face, no brain, but just a tail in front?

CASSANDRA: Brrrrt
Brrrrt
Zsssssssaa zsssssa
Brrrrrrt.

ORAL: You must always speak well of me.

CASSANDRA: SsssssssST!

ORAL: You must always praise me.

CASSANDRA: Brrrrt
brrrrt
zssssssBrrrrrt
ZsssBrrrrt.

ORAL: Yes, Yes, Yes. I know you know what I did so you better say the opposite. That nothing happened in this office.

CASSANDRA: Zzzzzzzzbbrrrrrt!
Sssssssssspft!

ORAL: Years from now, wherever you work, whatever you say about me, I will be listening. I have the power. I can do it. I will do it. You know this. Ms Jackson.

(CASSANDRA is silent.)

(SCATWOMAN becomes silent for the first time in this scene
All are quiet for a few beats.)

ORAL: (Peering closely at her) Is it the light? Is it your silence, or are you really pretty?

LILLI: (Singing off-stage)
Swallow and Nightingale
Were humans back in Greece.
Till bad king Oral
While on his throne

Ravished one,
Ripped out her tongue,
And changed both into birds!

Fly away, fly away, fly away girls
While bad king Oral
Is on his throne
Never your tale known.

Swallow with your strangled cries
An ox is on your tongue
Gurgle your tale of ancient crimes
Gurgle the horrors of present times
While your sister Nightingale
Chirps of your rape
In a lilting song.

Fly away, fly away, fly away girls
Never your tale heard.
While bad king Oral
Is on his throne
Never your tale known.

(LILLI *appears on stage as she finishes her song.)*

ORAL: Go away.

LILLI: I just got here.

*(Tries to gain entrance as* ORAL *blocks her)*

LILLI: Cassandra? Where are you? What's going on? Can you hear me?

ORAL: This office is closed. Go away! What's going on between you two anyhow?

LILLI: *(Struggling with* ORAL*)* Let me in!

ORAL: No!

LILLI: Yes

ORAL: No!

LILLI: Yes!

ORAL: *(Grabs and overpowers* LILLI*)* Oh bitch, puulease!

*(*SCATWOMAN *continues cleaning and humming.* CASSANDRA *runs confusedly in and out of the cage.)*

LILLI: *(Blasts* ORAL *in the face with her words)* A to Z! You asinine boldfaced creep you demented egotical excrement you fucking grinning hypocrite you impotent knockneed jackass you leching moronic nauseous overfed perverted rancid slimy turd unflushed vulgar weak yellow-throated zero! LET ME IN!

*(*ORAL *falls back, overwhelmed by the blast of words.)*

LILLI: *(Running toward* CASSANDRA*)* What the...Cassandra...TALK TO ME! What are you doing in this cage? O my God. The cage. Your dream.

*(*CASSANDRA *crawls out of the cage toward* LILLI*.)*

ORAL: There's no chains on her! Do you see any chains?

LILLI: *(To* CASSANDRA*)*
SPEAK TO ME!
*(To* SCATWOMAN*)*
Ma'am. What's happened? What's going on here?

ORAL: She's fired! She doesn't work here anymore. She doesn't count!

*(*SCATWOMAN *scoops water from her bucket and sprinkles it around like "holy water" as she continues her litany.)*

ORAL: *(To* LILLI*)* Before you came everything was just fine.

LILLI: *(To* CASSANDRA*)* Look at me. Talk. Your life depends on it. What's happening in here? Say something. Clear, simple, everyday words like b-a-s-t-a-r-d.

*(Enunciating slowly and carefully as* CASSANDRA *makes an effort to imitate her)*

LILLI: That's right. Come on. "M-o-t-h-e-r-f-u-c-k-e-r-"
Don't be afraid.

CASSANDRA: *(Face and body contorted in a painful effort to speak)*
MMMMmmmmmmMMMMMM—

ORAL: *She* doesn't need *you* to tell her how and what to say.

LILLI: *(Continues trying to teach* CASSANDRA, *who is making an attempt to repeat after her)* F-u-c-k-e-r.

CASSANDRA: Ffffffuuuuuuuuuu
ffuuuuuuuuu
uuuuuuuuu
Brrrrrrr.

LILLI: That's right! SPEAK! Your life depends on it! Open wide... AsssssssHolllllle.

ORAL: Shut up, Harpie! I'm sick of your mystic babble and psycho dribble.

CASSANDRA: AHHHHHHHHSSSSSSSSSSH Hoooohooohooo.

LILLI: *(Coaching CASSANDRA)* Assssshole. That's right. Open your mouth wide and breathe into the word. C'mon now—AssssssHooooole.

*(CASSANDRA is silent.)*

ORAL: *(Laughing)* She's not going to tell you anything.

LILLI: *(Desperately continues her lesson)* Press your lips together. Make the P sound P-P-P- like in P-e-r-v-e-r-t.

*(CASSANDRA remains silent. SCATWOMAN begins a low, elongated dance toward CASSANDRA and sings a slow chant. She pauses in front of CASSANDRA, and they stare at each other silently for several beats. Then SCATWOMAN silently lays her hand on CASSANDRA's lips.)*

CASSANDRA: *(Kneels before SCATWOMAN gurgling, desperately trying to form words)*
Rrrrrrrrrrrrrrr
Rrrrrrrrrrrrrrrrrrrrrrrr
Rrrrrrrrrrrrrrrrrrr.

*(SCATWOMAN resumes scatting and dances toward window.)*

CASSANDRA: *(Follows SCATWOMAN, still trying to speak)*
RrrrrrrrrrRRRRRR Aaaaaaaa Rrrrrrr AaaaaaHHH Rrrr Aaaa.

LILLI: SPEAK!

ORAL: Shut up! This is between *us. You* can't help here. You're too—

LILLI: Too pale? Don't be too sure.

ORAL: I bet you have hair on your chest! I bet you wear a jock strap! I bet you shave off your beard.

LILLI: *(Angrily thrusting a bare breast at ORAL)* You can bet I'm a woman. Do these look man-made? But don't let my tits stop me from recognizing a pervert when I see one.

*(SCATWOMAN begins a climbing scat as she sprinkles water on her own head and climbs upon the window sill.)*

LILLI: The bliss radiating from her eyes is blinding. She's shed her human tongue. She's talking with her ancestors.

SCATWOMAN: *(Possessed by the voice of Louis Armstrong)*
SHhhhhhhh!
Coronet the enemy
till they bleed
Twelve-bar blues
B Flat
B Sharp
B born on the 4th of July
Shoo be dooo
Ooo ya coo
Ooo bop she bam!
Dolly!

ORAL: You looney tune! You crackpot! Get down from that windowsill!

*(SCATWOMAN ominously points a finger at ORAL.)*

ORAL: *(Falling back, truly frightened)* DON'T POINT AT ME! My ma ain't dead.

SCATWOMAN: AEeeeeebop shebop blip de bop
Blue deschoo d shoo la sop
Swallow Eater!
I put a curse on you!
Mop demop Øoole mo
I put a curse on you!
Swallow eater
Feasting on slit lips
Festering tongues
Of silence
I put a curse you
May your sisters despise you
May your clerks ridicule you
May your wife divorce you
I put a curse on you
May the Spirit of Justice
Marshall all the Fiends of your injustice against you
May your Right arm wither
May Your Left arm grow
As you eternally
carry the burden of your lies

Up the Hill of Eternity forever!
She bamshe bom plie so ooahhde blipblue!

ORAL: *(Terrifed, trying to shield himself from* SCATWOMAN's *pointing finger)* Agghhhhhh!

SCATWOMAN: *(Turning toward* CASSANDRA*)*
Forget about mask and masquerade
Forget grunts and growls
No more moans and wiggles
No more secret codes
to an accompaniment of pain
Forget shoo be do
oo aya oo
sholooobedo oyya coo and bibpp de dahf boogie
Move on SPeak Out move on SPea move on speak out Speak, speak,
SpeakSPEAKSPEAK SPEAK SPEAKKKKSKKkkkkkkkkK!
*(Her voice crescendoes into a climax as she jumps out the window.)*

CASSANDRA: *(A slow, eerie sound, part bird, part woman, a sound that rises and falls, that is both speech and howl, lament and cry, laugh and curse, that rises and drones, flashes, stutters, and flows.)*
AHA AHA A HA AH AH A AHA AH AHA RRRRR
ARRRRRRRAAAAAAAAPPPPPPPPPPPPPPEEEEEEEEEEEEEEEEE.

ORAL: MOMMA AAAAAMAAAAAAAA—

LILLI: NOOH MY GODdddd OGPDOGODNO! NOOOOO MYGOD
NO OHHH MY GOD!

CASSANDRA: *(Stares after* SCATWOMAN, *her mouth working furiously to form the word as she now whispers.)*
RrrAaaPppEee...

ORAL: *(Becomes incoherent and mumbles to himself repeatedly)*
MOMMA, MOMMA, MOMMAMOMMA! I loved my Mama.
Mamma. Mamma.

LILLI: Your own mother?

CASSANDRA: *(Soft and timid)* RaaPPeeee

ORAL: *(Becoming more incoherent)*
Mmmmmammmma. S-sssSpeak to meeeeE. MmmmmmmMAMA.
Mamma. Mamma I'm allLLLalone here.

CASSANDRA: *(Whispering)* Rape.

LILLI: Louder please. Can't hear you.

ORAL: *(Still weeping, trying to ignore* CASSANDRA*)*
I'm notttttaa baddddd mmmman.

CASSANDRA: *(Pointing to* ORAL*)* Rape.

LILLI: Still can't hear you.

ORAL: *(Still weeping)* I pray. I'm a good man.

LILLI: I can't hear you.

CASSANDRA: Rape!

LILLI: Louder please. Didn't quite get it, Cassandra.

ORAL: I read my Bible.

CASSANDRA: Rape.

ORAL: I even listen to religious tapes.

CASSANDRA: *(Each word, though slowly and painfully formed, becomes clearer)* Hink I mmm mmmpffhh
Aha aha aha ha ha
*(Calling after* SCATWOMAN*)*
Your rage is in me
You spoke to me
In ways I could not hear
I would not, could not speak
You blessed me
Do you still bless me
Do you?

ORAL: You think you're a normal person now, don't you? In your own mind you are speaking clearly but to the rest of us it sounds like your same old gibberish.

CASSANDRA: Rape! Rape! Rape!
"You will speak the truth
that no one will want to believe
Not Father, Mother, Sister,
Not My People.
There is no rape among us.
She who cries 'rape'
Works against us
Dishonors our House
Discredits the race."

I swallow
Swallow words
Swallow agony

ORAL: Don't say this. Please don't saythis, Sister. Sister, don't
dooooothiiisSister.... ssssister.

CASSANDRA: Father refuses me his shelter.
Mother turns deaf against me.
They are defending
Everything we no longer have.

The more it fades away
The more Real
They say it is.

ORAL: Bring a man down...step all over a Brother's back.

CASSANDRA: I swallow
swallow
Swallow Agony
damn, damn damn damn

ORAL: *(Slowly, as if explaining to a child)* You-are-not-a-Greek-princess.
You-don't-live-in-ancient-Greece. You-are-only-in-America.
You-never-had-the-gift-of-prophecy.
You-don't-know-about-your-past-and-nobody-wants-to-hear-about-
you-now!

CASSANDRA: I feel no more sorry for myself
Than all the others.
Scatwoman and all the others.

You feed on us
You belch with our pain.
You are bloated with our lives.

Scatwoman
Your rage
Is in me
You tried to help
I did not know
You blessed me
I would not speak
Do you still bless me?
Scatwoman,
Do you?

Damn you Apollo
Damn damn you Tereus
Goddamn damn you Oral.
Oral, Oral Oral Oral.

ORAL: *(In the empty voice of a stuck robot)*
You-think-you're-a-normal-person-now-don't-you?
In-your-own-mind-you're-speaking-clearly-but-to-the-
rest-of-us-it-sounds-like-your-same-old-gibberish.

LILLI: Sounds perfectly clear to me.

ORAL: *(Continues in empty robotlike voice, repeating three times as he points at LILLI)* SsssShe-doesn't-want-to-help-youuuu.
Can't-you-see-her-sly-smile-her-hot-looks-her-pale-skin-her-long-silk-hair? *(He repeats six times.)*

LILLI: I think you should kill the bastard!

ORAL: What gives you the right???

LILLI: The Spirit that gives me the gifts of healing and interpretation, the Spirit that tells me that we should have the same care for one another, the Spirit that tells me that when one woman is dishonored, all are, that same Spirit tells me to say, "I think you should kill the bastard!"

*(ORAL mocks CASSANDRA with gurgling noises, sticking fingers in his ear and babbling throughout the following:)*

CASSANDRA: RAPE!
sly
impersonal,
pervasive
invading my
head
eyes
filling up my spaces
RAPE!
Attacking
without touching
RAPE/words
RAPE/games
RAPE/pictures
RAPE peace
RAPE pride

RAPE spirit
RAPE dignity
RAPE joy
RAPE trust
RAPE speech
All ravaged
all plundered
all gone
RAPE!
Lunch time,
Coffee time
RAPE!
in the bushes
under the stairs
in the office
worthless
slut
sister
worker
welfare
uppity
lesbian
feminist
whore
dyke
bitch
cunt
ambitious
matriarch
ugly
lazy
dumb
strong
fat
smart
lawyer
Traitor
educated
illiterate
dark skinned
Brother? brother? brother? brother?

Brother? brother? brother? brother?
Damn! damn! damn! damn! Goddamn!

ORAL: You-are-not-a-Greek-princess. You-don't-live-in-ancient
Greece. You-are-only-in-America. You-never-had-the-gift-of
prophecy-and-No-one-believes-any-thing-you-have-to-say.

CASSANDRA: I see Mammon
Running wild among us.
I see violence
Against dark women
Oppressed men
Downpressing oppressed women

ORAL: What nonsense!

CASSANDRA: Look!
I see violence
Against dark women
An initiation rite
Into white manhood.

I see violence against dark women
The great equalizer
Uniting black and white men
In a masculine dance.

ORAL: O Shut up you silly Lesbian and go put on some lipstick!

CASSANDRA: Now! Look!
Now I see
A sixty-seven-year-old grandmother
The first blast tears off her right arm
The one she bends at the elbow
As she embroiders handkerchiefs for friends.
The second blast blows out her heart
That soars every Sunday
At St Luke's A M E
As she sings "Precious Lord."
Shotgunned by rent marshals
Who won't bother to
Cover her naked body
As they carry her from her kitchenette
Down six flights of stairs

Past gawking neighbors
Into the Bronx streets.

I see my sister Theodora
Lying in the fetid halls of Harlem Hospital
Dying from an abusive husband
Who is cursing her deathbed
Angry because soon
She will be free.

I see my mother
On her way to St Martin's
In her Sunday hat
Offered two dollars
From a police car window.

ORAL: This is some dated, militant, sixties rubbish!

CASSANDRA: Now look! See over there!
In the Land of Providence.
I see my breast surgeon
Abrupt, cold, and rude
Avoiding my eyes
And "forgetting" to show up for my biopsy.

I see generations upon generations
Of young women,
becoming old women
without men,
Successfully raising their children alone
And bad mouthed for it.

I see Brothers
imitating Massa
sneaking from the White House
searching for Sista

For Black is beautiful
Only under night cover.

And Glory Hallelujah!
I see my Sisters loving
themselves,
Loving each other,
Loving whoever loves them.

ORAL: *(Becoming increasingly incoherent)* Wallow in the past. Gotta unnerstan I'm only a man. Thinkin' only of yourself strong you can take it. Take it like a man act like a woman queen of the Nile money maker booty shaker nationhood whattabout myALWAYS getta job manhood black woman has always Got MY job sho' nuffmoney maker 'tween legsbeen liberated, black is bootiful blonde is betterstrong, take it like a man male bashing blackpussywoman-bootiiefreelikeeamouth SHUTUPbootieie psuussygive gottahave itt shUT UPSHUTUPshhhut uppppppp.

CASSANDRA: Now! Look! See!
Helen Johnson thrown from the roof in New York City
Not a word in the papers.
Melanie Davis raped.
in a St John's Frat House
and dismissed for it.
Thirteen-year-old Ebony Williams raped and burned
Identified only by her charm bracelet.

Listen!
I hear brown-eyed, five-feet-and-two-inches Roxanne Jones,
Serving life imprisonment
For killing her wife-beating husband,
Six-feet-five, two-hundred-fifty pounds
Professional football player
as she cries
"What court could conduct a fair trial?
He is a man, an oppressed man
And I am only an
Un-Fair woman."

I know that you wish I were dumb again
But my Tongue refuses to be
Silent and buried alive
With the Liars.
Only I can describe the world I live in
Only I can describe
The life I've come to live
Only I can describe the men I need protection from.
I'm sick of the excuses.
It is not a racist society,
It is not a capitalistic system,
That has a gun in my head.

It is not a sexist culture,
That has a fist in my face,
A penis inside of me
Against my will.
Is there nothing left to describe the world
But the Silence of the Past?
Is the language of the Present
Too painful to hear?
Who will find a voice?
And when?
I think
I think I know
I think I decide
I think I'm in charge
I think I mean something
I think I must
I think I want to
I think I will
In known tongues
Speak out!

END OF PLAY

www.ingramcontent.com/pod-product-compliance
Lightning Source LLC
Chambersburg PA
CBHW070035110426
42741CB00035B/2780